EMMANUEL JOSEPH

The Tomorrow Architects, Billionaires Who Shape Industries and Rewrite the Rules of Power

Copyright © 2025 by Emmanuel Joseph

All rights reserved. No part of this publication may be reproduced, stored or transmitted in any form or by any means, electronic, mechanical, photocopying, recording, scanning, or otherwise without written permission from the publisher. It is illegal to copy this book, post it to a website, or distribute it by any other means without permission.

First edition

This book was professionally typeset on Reedsy.
Find out more at reedsy.com

Contents

1. Chapter 1: The Blueprint of Vision — 1
2. Chapter 2: The Rise of the Maverick — 3
3. Chapter 3: The Power of Influence — 5
4. Chapter 4: The Art of Strategic Alliances — 7
5. Chapter 5: The Role of Technology — 9
6. Chapter 6: The Innovation Ecosystem — 11
7. Chapter 7: The Pursuit of Sustainability — 13
8. Chapter 8: The Global Perspective — 15
9. Chapter 9: The Philanthropic Imperative — 17
10. Chapter 10: The Legacy of Leadership — 19
11. Chapter 11: The Ethical Compass — 21
12. Chapter 12: The Resilience Factor — 23
13. Chapter 13: The Cultural Impact — 25
14. Chapter 14: The Data Advantage — 27
15. Chapter 15: The Network Effect — 29
16. Chapter 16: The Future of Innovation — 31
17. Chapter 17: The Legacy of Impact — 33

1

Chapter 1: The Blueprint of Vision

In the dawn of every great industry, there exists a visionary whose dreams defy the limitations of the present. These individuals are the architects of tomorrow, seeing opportunities where others see obstacles. Visionaries like Elon Musk dare to dream of interplanetary colonization and renewable energy dominance, cultivating an environment of innovation that pushes their teams to think beyond conventional limits. By prioritizing long-term impact over short-term gains, they set the stage for transformative change, leaving an indelible mark on their respective industries.

Through the lens of their vision, we witness the birth of groundbreaking concepts that shape the future. These billionaires embrace the unknown, willing to invest time and resources into ventures that others deem too risky or impractical. Their ability to foresee market needs before they manifest positions them as pioneers of new frontiers. They inspire their teams to challenge the status quo, fostering a culture of creativity and experimentation. As a result, they bring to life revolutionary ideas that redefine entire industries.

Visionary billionaires possess an unwavering belief in their ideas, even when faced with skepticism and opposition. They understand that true innovation requires persistence and resilience. By staying true to their vision, they navigate through challenges and setbacks, emerging stronger and more determined. Their journey is a testament to the power of conviction and the impact of visionary leadership.

The blueprint of vision is not just about having big ideas; it is about the relentless pursuit of those ideas and the unwavering commitment to making them a reality. These billionaires demonstrate that the future belongs to those who dare to dream and have the courage to turn those dreams into reality.

2

Chapter 2: The Rise of the Maverick

Breaking the mold is a defining trait of the maverick billionaire. These trailblazers challenge the status quo and disrupt traditional business models. Steve Jobs revolutionized technology with his unrelenting pursuit of perfection, reimagining personal computing and mobile devices. Mavericks possess an innate ability to foresee market needs before they manifest, positioning themselves as pioneers of new frontiers. Their unconventional strategies often draw skepticism, but their unwavering belief in their vision propels them to unprecedented success. By embracing risk and defying norms, these billionaires carve out unique paths that redefine entire industries.

Mavericks are not afraid to take bold risks and challenge established norms. They thrive on pushing boundaries and exploring uncharted territories. Their ability to think differently and challenge conventional wisdom sets them apart as innovators and disruptors. They are willing to take risks that others shy away from, knowing that great rewards often come from bold decisions.

These trailblazers are driven by a relentless pursuit of excellence and a desire to create something truly remarkable. They are not satisfied with mediocrity and constantly strive for perfection. Their attention to detail and commitment to quality are evident in every aspect of their work. They inspire their teams to reach new heights and achieve extraordinary results.

The rise of the maverick is a story of defiance and determination. It is about challenging the status quo and daring to dream big. These billionaires prove that true innovation requires courage and a willingness to take risks. They show us that by embracing unconventional strategies and thinking outside the box, we can achieve greatness and reshape entire industries.

3

Chapter 3: The Power of Influence

Billionaires wield immense power, not just through their wealth, but through their influence. Warren Buffett, known as the Oracle of Omaha, exemplifies the profound impact of influence in the world of finance. His investment philosophies and ethical principles have shaped the strategies of countless investors worldwide. The ability to influence extends beyond business; it permeates cultural, social, and political realms. Influential billionaires leverage their platforms to advocate for change, champion causes, and inspire future generations. Their words and actions reverberate across society, molding public opinion and steering the course of industries.

Influence is a powerful tool that can shape the direction of entire industries. Billionaires who wield this influence understand the responsibility that comes with it. They use their platforms to raise awareness about important issues, drive positive change, and inspire others to take action. Their influence extends beyond their businesses, impacting society as a whole.

These influential billionaires are not content with simply accumulating wealth; they strive to make a difference in the world. They use their resources and platforms to support causes they are passionate about, from education and healthcare to environmental sustainability. Their philanthropic efforts create a ripple effect, inspiring others to contribute and make a positive impact.

The power of influence is not limited to financial success; it is about using one's platform to effect meaningful change. Influential billionaires understand that their actions and words have the potential to shape public opinion and drive societal progress. By leveraging their influence, they create a legacy that extends far beyond their businesses, leaving a lasting impact on the world.

4

Chapter 4: The Art of Strategic Alliances

Forging strategic alliances is a hallmark of industry-shaping billionaires. Partnerships with key players amplify their reach and accelerate their vision. Jeff Bezos transformed e-commerce by establishing symbiotic relationships with countless retailers and service providers. Strategic alliances create ecosystems of collaboration, where mutual interests converge to drive innovation and growth. These alliances extend beyond corporate boundaries, encompassing governments, non-profits, and academia. By fostering collaboration, billionaires harness collective expertise and resources, catalyzing progress on a grand scale. Through strategic alliances, they create a network of influence that sustains their impact.

Strategic alliances are essential for achieving long-term success and sustainability. Billionaires who master the art of forming these alliances understand the value of collaboration and mutual benefit. They seek out partners who share their vision and goals, creating a synergy that drives innovation and growth.

These alliances go beyond traditional business partnerships, encompassing a diverse range of stakeholders. By collaborating with governments, non-profits, and academic institutions, billionaires tap into a wealth of knowledge and resources. This collaborative approach enables them to address complex challenges and drive systemic change.

The art of strategic alliances lies in the ability to identify and nurture relationships that align with one's vision and goals. Billionaires who excel in this area create ecosystems of collaboration that amplify their impact and extend their reach. Through strategic alliances, they build a network of influence that sustains their success and drives long-term growth.

5

Chapter 5: The Role of Technology

Technology is the cornerstone of modern industry, and billionaires recognize its transformative power. Mark Zuckerberg's creation of Facebook revolutionized social connectivity, reshaping how we communicate and share information. These visionaries embrace emerging technologies, from artificial intelligence to blockchain, to drive their ventures forward. They invest heavily in research and development, fueling innovation that propels their industries into the future. The integration of technology not only enhances efficiency but also opens new avenues for growth and disruption. Billionaires who master technology position themselves at the forefront of industry evolution.

Technology is a powerful tool that has the potential to revolutionize entire industries. Billionaires who harness its potential understand the importance of staying ahead of technological advancements. They invest heavily in research and development, exploring new technologies and innovations that drive their businesses forward.

These visionaries embrace emerging technologies and integrate them into their operations, enhancing efficiency and productivity. They leverage artificial intelligence, blockchain, and other cutting-edge technologies to create new opportunities for growth and disruption. By staying ahead of technological trends, they position themselves as leaders in their industries.

The role of technology is not just about enhancing existing operations; it is about creating new possibilities and driving innovation. Billionaires who master technology understand that it is a powerful tool that can propel their businesses into the future. By embracing technological advancements, they ensure their continued success and influence in an ever-evolving world.

6

Chapter 6: The Innovation Ecosystem

Building an innovation ecosystem is essential for sustained industry leadership. Larry Page and Sergey Brin fostered a culture of innovation at Google, where creativity and experimentation thrive. Billionaires create environments that encourage risk-taking, where failure is seen as a stepping stone to success. They attract top talent by offering autonomy and opportunities for personal growth. Innovation ecosystems extend beyond the confines of a single company, encompassing startups, accelerators, and research institutions. By nurturing a vibrant ecosystem, billionaires ensure a continuous pipeline of groundbreaking ideas and technologies.

Innovation is the lifeblood of industry leadership. Billionaires who build vibrant innovation ecosystems understand the importance of fostering a culture of creativity and experimentation. They create environments that encourage risk-taking and view failure as a learning opportunity.

These innovation ecosystems attract top talent by offering autonomy and opportunities for personal growth. Billionaires who prioritize innovation understand that their success depends on the collective efforts of their teams. They provide the resources and support needed to nurture groundbreaking ideas and technologies.

Innovation ecosystems extend beyond the boundaries of a single company. They encompass startups, accelerators, and research institutions, creating a network of collaboration and mutual support. By nurturing this ecosystem, billionaires ensure a continuous pipeline of innovative ideas that drive their industries forward.

7

Chapter 7: The Pursuit of Sustainability

Sustainability is a driving force for billionaires committed to shaping industries responsibly. Elon Musk's ventures into electric vehicles and solar energy exemplify the pursuit of sustainable solutions. These billionaires recognize the imperative to balance profitability with environmental stewardship. They invest in green technologies, circular economies, and carbon reduction initiatives. Sustainability is not just a moral obligation; it is a strategic advantage that resonates with conscious consumers and investors. By championing sustainability, billionaires contribute to a healthier planet while securing long-term viability for their industries.

Sustainability is a critical component of responsible industry leadership. Billionaires who prioritize sustainability understand the importance of balancing profitability with environmental stewardship. They invest in green technologies and initiatives that reduce their carbon footprint and promote a circular economy.

These billionaires recognize that sustainability is not just a moral obligation; it is a strategic advantage. Consumers and investors are increasingly conscious of the environmental impact of businesses, and companies that prioritize sustainability are more likely to gain their trust and support.

The pursuit of sustainability is about creating a healthier planet and ensuring the long-term viability of industries. Billionaires who champion sustainability understand that their success is intertwined with the success of industries. By adopting sustainable practices, they ensure a positive impact on the environment and contribute to the well-being of future generations.

8

Chapter 8: The Global Perspective

Industry-shaping billionaires operate with a global perspective, understanding the interconnectedness of economies and societies. Jack Ma's Alibaba transformed e-commerce not just in China but globally, bridging markets and cultures. These billionaires navigate complex geopolitical landscapes, adapting their strategies to diverse regulatory environments. They seize opportunities in emerging markets, driving economic development and uplifting communities. A global perspective enables billionaires to anticipate trends and challenges, positioning them as agile leaders in an ever-changing world. Their ability to think globally ensures their impact transcends borders.

A global perspective is essential for billionaires who seek to shape industries and make a lasting impact. These visionary leaders understand the interconnectedness of economies and societies, recognizing that their actions can have far-reaching consequences. By adopting a global mindset, they navigate complex geopolitical landscapes and adapt their strategies to diverse regulatory environments.

Billionaires with a global perspective seize opportunities in emerging markets, driving economic development and uplifting communities. They understand that growth is not confined to their home countries and actively seek to expand their influence on a global scale. By bridging markets and cultures, they create a more interconnected and inclusive world.

The ability to think globally enables billionaires to anticipate trends and challenges, positioning them as agile leaders in an ever-changing world. They stay ahead of the curve by understanding the global landscape and leveraging their resources to drive innovation and growth. Their impact transcends borders, shaping industries and influencing societies worldwide.

9

Chapter 9: The Philanthropic Imperative

Philanthropy is a powerful tool for billionaires to effect positive change beyond their industries. Bill Gates' foundation addresses global health and education challenges, leveraging his wealth for societal betterment. Philanthropic initiatives extend the influence of billionaires, addressing systemic issues and fostering equitable growth. They collaborate with governments, NGOs, and grassroots organizations to amplify their impact. Philanthropy reflects their commitment to leaving a legacy that transcends business success. By prioritizing social responsibility, billionaires align their wealth with a higher purpose, driving transformative change on a global scale.

Philanthropy is an essential component of responsible leadership for billionaires who seek to make a positive impact on the world. These visionary leaders use their wealth and resources to address pressing social issues, from global health and education to environmental sustainability. By leveraging their influence, they create lasting change that extends beyond their industries.

Philanthropic initiatives reflect the commitment of billionaires to leaving a legacy that transcends business success. They collaborate with governments, NGOs, and grassroots organizations to amplify their impact and address systemic issues. Their efforts drive equitable growth and create opportunities for marginalized communities.

The philanthropic imperative is about aligning wealth with a higher purpose and using it to drive transformative change. Billionaires who prioritize social responsibility understand that their success is not just measured by financial gains, but by the positive impact they have on society. By championing philanthropy, they create a lasting legacy that benefits future generations.

10

Chapter 10: The Legacy of Leadership

Leadership is the bedrock of billionaires who shape industries and rewrite the rules of power. Richard Branson's Virgin Group exemplifies visionary leadership, characterized by boldness and adaptability. These leaders inspire loyalty and dedication, fostering a culture of excellence. They lead by example, embodying the values and principles they espouse. Leadership extends beyond the confines of their companies, influencing broader industry standards and practices. Billionaires cultivate future leaders, mentoring and empowering the next generation to carry forward their vision. Their legacy of leadership endures, shaping the future of industries.

Leadership is a fundamental quality of billionaires who seek to make a lasting impact on their industries. These visionary leaders inspire loyalty and dedication by fostering a culture of excellence and innovation. They lead by example, embodying the values and principles they espouse, and creating an environment where their teams can thrive.

Billionaires with a legacy of leadership extend their influence beyond the confines of their companies. They set industry standards and practices, shaping the direction of entire sectors. Their leadership is characterized by boldness and adaptability, enabling them to navigate challenges and seize opportunities.

These leaders also recognize the importance of cultivating future leaders.

They mentor and empower the next generation, ensuring that their vision and values are carried forward. By investing in leadership development, they create a legacy that endures and shapes the future of industries.

11

Chapter 11: The Ethical Compass

Ethics play a pivotal role in the conduct of billionaires who shape industries. Howard Schultz's Starbucks is a testament to ethical business practices, prioritizing employee welfare and fair trade. These billionaires navigate ethical dilemmas with integrity, balancing profit motives with social responsibility. They uphold transparency, accountability, and ethical governance, setting benchmarks for industry standards. An ethical compass ensures trust and credibility, fostering long-term relationships with stakeholders. By adhering to ethical principles, billionaires create a positive impact that resonates with consumers, investors, and society at large.

Ethics are a cornerstone of responsible industry leadership. Billionaires who prioritize ethical business practices understand the importance of balancing profit motives with social responsibility. They navigate ethical dilemmas with integrity, upholding transparency, accountability, and ethical governance.

An ethical compass ensures trust and credibility, fostering long-term relationships with stakeholders. Billionaires who adhere to ethical principles set benchmarks for industry standards, creating a positive impact that resonates with consumers, investors, and society at large. Their commitment to ethics reflects their dedication to responsible leadership and sustainable success.

By prioritizing employee welfare, fair trade, and other ethical practices, these visionary leaders create a positive work environment and contribute to the well-being of their communities. Their actions inspire others to adopt ethical practices and drive positive change in their industries.

12

Chapter 12: The Resilience Factor

Resilience is a defining characteristic of billionaires who weather the storms of industry. Jeff Bezos' Amazon faced numerous challenges, yet his resilience turned setbacks into opportunities for growth. These billionaires possess unwavering determination, bouncing back from failures and adversities. They adapt to changing circumstances, demonstrating agility in the face of uncertainty. Resilience is fueled by a growth mindset, where challenges are viewed as learning experiences. By embracing resilience, billionaires navigate through crises, emerging stronger and more resilient. Their ability to persevere ensures their continued influence and impact.

Resilience is a crucial quality for billionaires who seek to make a lasting impact on their industries. These visionary leaders possess unwavering determination and the ability to bounce back from failures and adversities. They view challenges as learning experiences and adapt to changing circumstances with agility.

A growth mindset fuels resilience, enabling billionaires to navigate through crises and emerge stronger. Their ability to persevere ensures their continued influence and impact on their industries. By embracing resilience, they demonstrate the importance of staying committed to their vision and goals, even in the face of uncertainty.

The resilience factor is about turning setbacks into opportunities for growth and innovation. Billionaires who embody this quality inspire others to stay determined and focused on their goals. Their resilience is a testament to their leadership and dedication to shaping the future of their industries.

13

Chapter 13: The Cultural Impact

Billionaires who shape industries often leave an indelible mark on culture. Walt Disney's empire not only revolutionized entertainment but also became an integral part of popular culture. These visionaries create brands and products that resonate deeply with consumers, transcending generations. Cultural impact extends beyond business success, influencing societal values, norms, and aspirations. Billionaires leverage their platforms to drive cultural conversations, shaping public discourse and trends. Their contributions to culture enrich lives, fostering a sense of connection and identity. The cultural legacy of billionaires endures, leaving an everlasting imprint on society.

Cultural impact is a powerful aspect of industry leadership. Billionaires who shape industries create brands and products that resonate deeply with consumers, transcending generations. Their contributions to culture influence societal values, norms, and aspirations, creating a lasting legacy.

These visionary leaders leverage their platforms to drive cultural conversations and shape public discourse. They use their influence to address important issues, raise awareness, and inspire change. Their cultural impact extends beyond business success, enriching lives and fostering a sense of connection and identity.

The cultural legacy of billionaires endures, leaving an everlasting imprint on society. Their contributions to culture create a positive impact that resonates with future generations, shaping the values and aspirations of individuals and communities.

14

Chapter 14: The Data Advantage

In the age of information, data is a powerful asset for billionaires who shape industries. Satya Nadella's leadership at Microsoft underscores the strategic importance of data-driven decision-making. These billionaires harness the power of big data and analytics to gain insights, predict trends, and optimize operations. Data-driven strategies enable them to make informed decisions, identify opportunities, and mitigate risks. By leveraging data, billionaires create personalized experiences for consumers, enhancing satisfaction and loyalty. The data advantage positions them at the forefront of industry innovation, driving efficiency and growth.

Data is a valuable asset for billionaires who seek to make a lasting impact on their industries. These visionary leaders harness the power of big data and analytics to gain insights, predict trends, and optimize operations. Data-driven decision-making enables them to make informed choices, identify opportunities, and mitigate risks.

By leveraging data, billionaires create personalized experiences for consumers, enhancing satisfaction and loyalty. The data advantage positions them at the forefront of industry innovation, driving efficiency and growth. Their ability to harness the power of data sets them apart as leaders in an increasingly data-driven world.

The data advantage is about using information to drive strategic decisions and create value. Billionaires who master this aspect of leadership understand the importance of staying ahead of technological advancements and leveraging data to drive their businesses forward. Their data-driven strategies ensure their continued success and influence in an ever-evolving world.

15

Chapter 15: The Network Effect

The network effect is a key driver of success for billionaires who shape industries. Reid Hoffman's LinkedIn exemplifies the exponential growth achieved through network dynamics. These visionaries create platforms and ecosystems that thrive on interconnectedness, where each new user enhances the value for others. The network effect accelerates adoption, scalability, and market dominance. Billionaires build communities of users, partners, and stakeholders, fostering collaboration and engagement. The network effect not only amplifies their reach but also reinforces their influence, creating a self-sustaining cycle of growth and impact.

The network effect is a powerful driver of success for billionaires who create platforms and ecosystems. These visionary leaders understand the importance of interconnectedness and leverage it to achieve exponential growth. They build communities of users, partners, and stakeholders, fostering collaboration and engagement.

By creating platforms that thrive on the network effect, billionaires accelerate adoption, scalability, and market dominance. Each new user enhances the value for others, creating a self-sustaining cycle of growth and impact. The network effect amplifies their reach and reinforces their influence, positioning them as leaders in their industries.

The network effect is about creating a virtuous cycle of growth and engagement. Billionaires who harness this dynamic understand the power of interconnectedness and leverage it to drive their businesses forward. Their ability to build thriving ecosystems ensures their continued success and influence.

16

Chapter 16: The Future of Innovation

Billionaires who shape industries are perpetual innovators, always looking to the future. Elon Musk's ventures into space exploration and neural interfaces exemplify the relentless pursuit of innovation. These visionaries anticipate technological advancements and societal shifts, positioning themselves ahead of the curve. They invest in cutting-edge research, explore uncharted territories, and pioneer new paradigms. The future of innovation is a canvas for billionaires to paint their visions, pushing the boundaries of what is possible. Their forward-thinking approach ensures their continued relevance and leadership in an ever-evolving world.

Innovation is the lifeblood of industry leadership, and billionaires who shape industries are perpetual innovators. These visionary leaders anticipate technological advancements and societal shifts, positioning themselves ahead of the curve. They invest in cutting-edge research, explore uncharted territories, and pioneer new paradigms.

The future of innovation is a canvas for billionaires to paint their visions, pushing the boundaries of what is possible. Their forward-thinking approach ensures their continued relevance and leadership in an ever-evolving world. By staying ahead of technological trends and societal changes, they drive progress and shape the future of their industries.

Billionaires who prioritize innovation understand that it is essential for sustained success and influence. They embrace new ideas and technologies, constantly seeking ways to improve and disrupt. Their commitment to innovation ensures that they remain at the forefront of industry evolution, driving change and shaping the future.

17

Chapter 17: The Legacy of Impact

The ultimate measure of a billionaire's success is the legacy of impact they leave behind. Oprah Winfrey's media empire has not only shaped entertainment but also empowered millions. These visionaries create enduring legacies that extend beyond their lifetimes, influencing future generations. The impact of their work transcends financial success, touching lives and communities in profound ways. Billionaires who shape industries leave a legacy of innovation, leadership, and positive change that continues to inspire and uplift.

The legacy of impact is the ultimate measure of a billionaire's success. These visionary leaders create enduring legacies that extend beyond their lifetimes, influencing future generations. Their work transcends financial success, touching lives and communities in profound ways.

Billionaires who shape industries leave a legacy of innovation, leadership, and positive change. They inspire and uplift others, creating a lasting impact that continues to resonate long after they are gone. Their contributions to society, culture, and industry create a ripple effect that benefits future generations.

The legacy of impact is about creating a lasting and meaningful contribution to the world. Billionaires who prioritize this aspect of leadership understand that their true success is measured by the positive change they create. Their enduring legacy serves as an inspiration and a testament to the power of visionary leadership.

In **"The Tomorrow Architects: Billionaires Who Shape Industries and Rewrite the Rules of Power,"** explore the riveting stories of visionary billionaires who have redefined the landscape of modern industries. Through their audacious dreams, relentless innovation, and unparalleled leadership, these mavericks have not only amassed immense wealth but also wielded extraordinary influence to shape the future.

This book delves into the minds of iconic figures such as Elon Musk, Steve Jobs, Warren Buffett, Jeff Bezos, and others, uncovering the secrets behind their groundbreaking successes. Learn how they transformed challenges into opportunities, forged strategic alliances, and harnessed the power of technology to drive their ventures forward.

"The Tomorrow Architects" illuminates the ethical compass, resilience, and cultural impact that define these trailblazers, while highlighting their commitment to sustainability and philanthropy. From revolutionizing e-commerce to championing renewable energy, these billionaires are the architects of tomorrow, leaving a legacy of innovation and positive change.

Join us on a journey through seventeen compelling chapters that celebrate the power of visionary leadership and the indelible mark left by those who dare to dream big.

www.ingramcontent.com/pod-product-compliance
Lightning Source LLC
LaVergne TN
LVHW020500080526
838202LV00057B/6057